DATE DUE

Bulimia

Perspectives on Mental Health

by Bonnie Graves

Consultant:
Claire Mysko
Administrative Director
American Anorexia Bulimia Association

LifeMatters
an imprint of Capstone Press
Mankato, Minnesota

C 1   2003   16.95

LifeMatters Books are published by Capstone Press
PO Box 669 • 151 Good Counsel Drive • Mankato, Minnesota 56002
http://www.capstone-press.com

Printed in the United States of America

Library of Congress Cataloging-in-Publication Data
Graves, Bonnie B.
     Bulimia / by Bonnie Graves
          p.   cm. — (Perspectives on mental health)
     Includes biographical references and index.
     Summary: Describes the causes and characteristics of bulimia and offers strategies for dealing with your own or others' bulimia.
     ISBN 0-7368-0430-7 (book) — ISBN 0-7368-0440-4 (series)
     1. Bulimia—Juvenile literature. 2. Eating disorders—Juvenile literature.
     [1. Bulimia. 2. Eating disorders.] I. Title. II. Series
     RC552.B84 G73 2000
     616.85′263—dc21   99-056059
                                                CIP

Staff Credits
Marta Fahrenz, editor; Adam Lazar, designer; Jodi Theisen, photo researcher

Photo Credits
Cover: ©Capstone Press/Adam Lazar
FPG International/©Ron Chapple, 19; ©Telegraph Colour Library, 43, 51; ©Steven W. Jones, 57
International Stock/©Mark Bolster, 11; ©Giovanni Lunardi, 15; ©Scott Barrow, 26; ©Laurie Bayer, 39
Photo Network/©Esbin-Anderson, 6, 34; ©Chad Ehlers, 22
Unicorn Stock/©Eric R. Berndt, 41
Uniphoto/©Bob Daemmrich, 7, 16; ©Rick Brady, 49; ©Llewellyn, 59
Visuals Unlimited/©Bill Beatty, 47; ©Jeff Greenberg, 54

A 0 9 8 7 6 5 4 3 2 1

Table of Contents

People who have eating disorders misuse food to try to manage uncomfortable feelings.

People eat food to satisfy both physical and emotional needs.

People with bulimia nervosa binge, eat, and then purge. Bingeing and purging is different for each person with bulimia.

Anorexia nervosa and compulsive overeating are two other types of eating disorders. People with anorexia starve themselves. People who compulsively overeat binge but do not purge.

Eating disorders are serious health conditions, but they can be prevented and cured.

Chapter 1

Food—Friend or Foe?

CALLIE, AGE 15

Callie slammed down the phone. Jason was mad at her. She couldn't stand it. She couldn't stand *anyone* being mad at her. Callie walked into the kitchen and pulled a big box of crackers from the cupboard. She ate the whole box. After she finished the crackers, she ate a bag of cookies. Then she topped it all off with a couple of pints of ice cream.

Why Do People Misuse Food?

Callie has an eating disorder. People with eating disorders misuse food. They eat too much or too little. Often they eat for the wrong reasons. People with eating disorders use food to try to manage uncomfortable feelings such as anger or helplessness.

Everyone misuses food once in a while. Who hasn't felt stressed out after a test or a fight with a parent? Some people might eat an entire pizza or bag of candy to deal with such stress. Others may lose their appetite for a few days. However, people with eating disorders misuse food often. They end up putting their health and life at risk.

Why Do We Need Food?

Think about why you eat. The answer probably seems obvious. Your body needs food to stay alive. Food is fuel that provides your body with energy to get through each day. Your body also uses food to grow and repair itself. It is hard-wired to know just how much food it needs.

Your brain needs food, too, but for different reasons. It needs food to help it develop and function properly. Your brain also finds pleasure, comfort, or security in food.

"Hey, we're having a pizza party Friday night. Can you come?"

"Sure. What can I bring?"

"How about dessert? Something chocolate!"

Think about your own favorite food. You like it because it tastes good, but you probably like it for other reasons, too. It may remind you of good times or people you like.

When your mind and body are working together, you usually eat the right food in the right amounts. However, sometimes things can go wrong. Your mind and emotions can lead you to misuse food. You might gobble up a chocolate cream pie because you're angry or sad. You might refuse your body the food it needs because you're afraid of being fat.

Bulimia means "ox hunger," which refers to the large amount of food eaten during bingeing.

Ashley pulled a bag of potato chips from their hiding place. "I'll eat just a few," she told herself. She ate one handful, then another and another. Before she knew it, she had finished the whole bag. She felt terrible. Her stomach hurt. She felt guilty for eating so much. All those chips would make her fat. But Ashley knew what she would do. She would get rid of what she had eaten. She would make herself throw up.

ASHLEY, AGE 17

Bulimia Nervosa

Ashley has an eating disorder called bulimia nervosa, or just bulimia. People with this disorder binge and purge. Bingeing is eating uncontrollably. After bingeing, the person usually experiences feelings of guilt and shame. Purging is ridding the body of food. Purging usually is done by vomiting, or throwing up. It also is done using laxatives, which are drugs that loosen and help to eliminate the body's waste quickly.

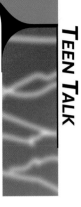
"I had just broken up with my boyfriend. I was feeling so lost and lonely. I just didn't know what to do, so I started eating. Then I started purging to get rid of what I'd eaten. I got into bingeing and purging and just couldn't stop."—Melanie, age 16

"I went through two exercise tapes a day. I felt guilty and fat when I didn't exercise two hours every day."
—Vannalay, age 15

Bingeing and purging is different for each person with bulimia. For example, not all people with bulimia gorge themselves. One person might consider a binge to be a single cookie. Another might binge on a two-pound box of chocolates.

People with bulimia are obsessed, or overly concerned, with both food and weight. They usually are dissatisfied with their body. They have a strong urge to overeat, which results in bingeing. Then they purge to try to prevent gaining weight after bingeing. People with bulimia also may exercise too much, use diet pills, or give themselves enemas. An enema forces liquid into the intestines to eliminate waste quickly.

Bulimia has increased at a greater rate than anorexia over the past five years. One study of high school students reported that 2.7 percent of girls and 1.4 percent of boys in the United States engage in bulimic behavior.

Other Eating Disorders

Bulimia affects up to 3 percent of young women in the United States. Two other eating disorders are anorexia nervosa and binge-eating disorder, which is sometimes called compulsive overeating.

People with anorexia are terrified of being fat, so they starve themselves. They have a strong need to control their weight. Along with starving themselves, they may exercise excessively. It is possible for a person to have both anorexia and bulimia.

Like people with bulimia, people who compulsively overeat gorge themselves on food. They eat rapidly and continue eating when they are full. Unlike people with bulimia, those who compulsively overeat do not purge themselves.

Eating disorders are serious health conditions. Often an eating disorder develops so gradually that people may not even know they have one. However, eating disorders can be prevented and cured. This book will help you learn how to prevent and cure bulimia.

Points to Consider

What are the differences between a person with bulimia and a person who compulsively overeats?

Why do you think eating disorders are considered mental health problems?

When you are depressed or angry, what do you do to make yourself feel better?

Do you think forced vomiting could be harmful? Why?

Chapter Overview

In today's culture, people are encouraged to eat more than their body needs. However, they also are told that they should be thin and fit.

Many times eating disorders start out as diets.

Females are at greater risk than males for eating disorders.

Teens especially feel the pressure to be thin. Sometimes this pressure can trigger an eating disorder.

Chapter **2**

Why Is It So Important to Be Thin?

Matt studied himself in the mirror. Fat! He was fat. There was no getting around it. He looked nothing, *nothing,* like the guys in magazines and on TV.

Well, that wasn't exactly true. He looked like an ordinary guy. He just didn't look like the popular guys.

MATT, AGE 14

"Just look at the people you see on TV and in the movies. Who has all the friends and success? Who is admired? Only the ones that look good, the ones who are thin. Is this a crock, or what?"—Derek, age 16

"Believe in yourself, not in some phony image made up by advertisers."—Lara, age 18

Food Versus Body Image

All of us need food to live. Most of us want food as well. We enjoy how it tastes and how it makes us feel. Food gives us comfort and pleasure.

At the same time, people are told to be thin. The message is: Thin people are beautiful, happy, and successful. Think about the models you see in fashion magazines. Most of them are stick thin. What about your favorite TV characters or movie stars? Are most of them thin? Today, thin women and lean men are held up as the ideal. Fat men and women often are made fun of.

Despite the messages to be thin, people are constantly being told to eat. Fast food is available on practically every corner. Almost every school and business has vending machines. Food jumps out from TV, billboards, and magazines. Whenever people get together, snacks and drinks are at their fingertips. Food is abundant at most parties.

Many people can't resist the constant pressure to eat. Often people consume more than they need. They end up choosing food over being thin. Obesity, the condition of being excessively overweight, is common in North America. In fact, over half of adult Americans are overweight.

Many people try dieting. Some are successful at losing weight. Others never lose the weight they want. Two-thirds of people who diet gain back the weight they lost within one year. Almost all people who diet will gain back the weight they lost within five years. Some people start dieting and can't stop. Those with bulimia eat and purge to try to stay thin.

Not everyone who diets has an eating disorder. However, most people with eating disorders have tried diets.

Women and Eating Disorders

Girls and women especially are at risk for eating disorders. About 90 to 95 percent of anorexia and bulimia occurs in females. Starting in their teen years or earlier, most girls feel pressure to have a lean figure. They see gorgeous actresses and models on TV, in movies, and in magazines. The successful, famous, beautiful people are almost always thin.

Sometimes these successful, famous people are thin because they have anorexia or bulimia. Certain activities or careers tend to include a high number of people who have eating disorders. Many athletes, gymnasts, dancers, skaters, models, and actors have anorexia or bulimia. People whose career depends on their body and face feel extreme pressure to be attractive and in shape. Some experts estimate that from 15 to 60 percent of athletes and performers have eating disorders. According to the American College of Sports Medicine, 62 percent of female athletes are at risk for an eating disorder.

Only about 5 to 10 percent of people with anorexia or bulimia are males. This may be because society expects men to be strong and powerful. Some men feel ashamed if their body is too thin. Women, however, are supposed to be tiny and thin.

Research suggests that about 50 percent of people who have had anorexia develop bulimia or bulimic patterns.

More men may have eating disorders than are reported. Males may hide an eating disorder because they believe only women have the problem. They may feel ashamed and embarrassed to admit they have an eating disorder.

MICHELLE, AGE 17

"Are you trying out for the gymnastics team?" Talia asked Michelle.

"I'd like to, but I think maybe I'm too fat."

"Well, you probably could lose a little weight. Have you thought about dieting?" Talia asked.

Michelle didn't tell Talia she had been dieting. How much less could she eat? She'd just have to start throwing up what she ate.

Bulimia is more likely to develop in the late teens. Anorexia usually develops between ages 12 and 17. Girls who start puberty early have a greater risk of bulimia.

Teen Girls Are at Risk

The teen years often are a time when people are dissatisfied with their body. Before puberty, the age of sexual maturity, boys and girls have about the same amount of body fat. At the end of puberty, girls often have twice as much body fat as before. This is a natural part of maturity. However, this is a time when many girls become obsessed with their weight.

Appearance counts to teens. In a national survey of 4,000 teens, 45 percent said they were unhappy with the way they looked. More than 60 percent said they felt a lot of pressure to have a perfect body. And 62 percent said that they were obsessed with their body. It is not surprising that eating disorders are on the rise.

Points to Consider

Explain why you agree or disagree with this statement: It's not how a person looks but what is inside that counts.

Why do you think so many people in our society eat too much?

Do you think a diet could turn into an eating disorder? Why?

Have you ever felt pressure to go on a diet? Where did the pressure come from? What did you do about it?

Chapter Overview

A culture that places a high value on thinness contributes to eating disorders.

People with bulimia may have personality traits such as low self-esteem and the tendency to avoid conflict. A high percentage have borderline personality disorder.

People with bulimia often have been abused as children. Many come from families in which there is substance abuse.

Teens feel pressure to fit in. They are dealing with lots of changes. Some use food as a way to take control of their life.

Chapter **3**

Looking at the Causes

Viv couldn't wait to get home from school. After that dumb

thing she said to Kari at lunch, she could never hang with that crowd again. Not one person cared about her. She knew it.

By the time she got home she was starving. She opened a big bag of chips. She ate the whole bag.

"No way am I going to let that bag of chips turn into more pounds," she told herself.

Should she vomit or take laxatives? She hated vomiting, but she couldn't take laxatives. She had a math test the next day. She wouldn't be able to sneak to the bathroom. But she couldn't gain weight. Being thin was all she had.

No Simple Answers

Why does bulimia develop in certain people and not in others? The answer isn't easy. Bulimia rarely has a single cause. As mentioned in chapter 2, TV, movies, and magazines give the message that being thin matters. However, there is more to it than that. People like Viv may have bulimia for many reasons. Personality traits, family, and life issues all can play a part.

Personality Traits

Certain personality traits have been found among people who have bulimia. Often people with bulimia have low self-esteem. They tend to avoid conflict. Many people with bulimia have borderline personality disorder.

Low Self-Esteem

People who have low self-esteem often don't feel valued or important. They may not like or respect themselves. They may think they are worthwhile only if other people like and approve of them. People with low self-esteem often feel guilty because they think they can't do anything right. Viv has low self-esteem. She thinks no one cares about her. Because Viv thinks that no one could like her for who she is inside, she has to look good. She has to be thin.

Four strong binge triggers are hunger, loneliness, anger, and fatigue. Feeling any one of these can trigger binge eating.

"For once would you get with the program, Trey? Can't I ever count on you? Can't you do anything right?"

TREY, AGE 14

Trey recalled his mom's words from that morning. Why couldn't he stick up for himself? He was such a wimp, never saying a word back. Now he'd eaten his fifth burger and second milkshake. All that remained was to get rid of them.

Fear of Conflict

People who fear or avoid conflict are afraid of their own and other people's anger. Conflict makes them so uncomfortable they will do almost anything to keep away from it. Even the smallest disagreement can be threatening to people who avoid conflict. They don't understand that conflict is normal and healthy. Sometimes they end up using food to hide from feelings rather than face an unpleasant situation.

Trey binges and purges instead of telling his mother how he really feels. He is attempting to cope with his fear of conflict. Bingeing and purging is his way of expressing shame, grief, and anger with his mother's criticism.

Overeating can alter brain chemistry. Overeating activates brain chemicals that produce feelings of peace and happiness. Some researchers believe people with bulimia may use food to self-medicate painful feelings.

Borderline Personality Disorder

Studies show that nearly 40 percent of people with bulimia have borderline personality disorder (BPD). These people tend to have extreme mood changes. They can go from being joyously happy to extremely angry in just a few hours. They often feel bored and empty, as though life just doesn't matter. People with BPD also have low self-esteem. They hate to be alone and want constant attention. Their fears and needs may lead them to misuse food.

Family Issues

People with bulimia often live in families in which alcohol or drug abuse is present. Children whose parents abuse drugs or alcohol may misuse food to block out painful feelings and emotions. Often children in these families feel out of control. They may use food as a way of gaining control.

Bulimia often occurs in people who have been abused as children. Sometimes people with bulimia blame themselves for the abuse. Bingeing and purging is a way to punish themselves.

Even young children are weight-conscious. Canadian children in grades 3 and 4 said they would rather lose a parent, get cancer, or live through nuclear war than be fat.

Children whose families have difficulty talking about feelings and emotions also are at risk for bulimia or other eating disorders. As teens, they may use bulimia as a way to express the feelings they were not allowed to show.

Research shows that parents can pass on traits to their children that may cause bulimia to develop. These inherited traits can include emotional or personality disorders. Children whose parent or parents have had bulimia have an increased risk for bulimia.

Life Issues

The teen years can be a stressful time. Teens must adapt to a changing body and new relationships. They often face challenging decisions. Most teens experience some changes and losses that add even more stress to their life. For example, moving to a new city or town or going to a new school can be a difficult change. Having a family member lose a job or become ill adds stress to daily life. A teen whose parents divorce goes through a life-changing experience. Breaking up with a girlfriend or boyfriend can feel like the end of the world. These situations leave a teen feeling lost and lonely. Food may seem like a best— or only—friend.

Pressure to fit in adds to the many physical and emotional changes that teens experience. Being part of a group sometimes is more important to teens than school or family. Teens want to be liked, to be popular. Some think being thin is a way to achieve this. Sometimes being thin becomes the most important thing in their life.

Everyone feels life is out of control sometimes. When this happens, some people turn to the one thing they can control—food. The problem is, food can end up being the controller. A destructive, life-threatening cycle can result. However, this cycle can be avoided.

"I thought if I was thinner I'd feel better about myself."
—Josiah, age 14

"My parents were always arguing. I hated it, but I never said anything. I just ate and ate."—Mara, age 15

"I wanted to look like the fashion models. I didn't realize that was impossible for me. I have big bones. There's no way I could change that. I could never get down to a size 5. I don't know why I thought I could. Guess I was brain-washed in a way. I don't buy fashion magazines anymore."—Georgia, age 17

Points to Consider

The current culture says thin women are beautiful. Do you agree? Why or why not?

Why might people with low self-esteem be at risk for bulimia?

Do you feel pressure to look or act a certain way? Where does this pressure come from? How do you deal with it?

Chapter Overview

Many people with bulimia hide their disorder well. Often they are of normal weight and act happy.

People with bulimia feel compelled to binge and purge.

Bingeing and purging provides temporary comfort to a person with bulimia.

People with bulimia realize their actions are not normal. Many are ashamed of their bingeing and purging.

A person who has bulimia feels caught in a trap. He or she wants to get out of it but can't.

Chapter **4**

Amy's Story

Kevin and Amy sat at a table in a candlelit restaurant. They were celebrating. They had been dating for a year. Amy smiled and touched Kevin's hand. How lucky she was to have a boyfriend like Kevin. Then Amy excused herself. She told Kevin she had to use the restroom.

Amy was gone a long time. When she came back to the table, her hair was combed. She was sucking on a breath mint. She sat down next to Kevin and smiled. Kevin had no idea Amy had bulimia.

KEVIN AND AMY, AGE 18

"I couldn't believe Jill had bulimia. I mean, she always acted so happy. She never told me how she really felt."
—Nina, age 14

"I felt so empty inside and really sad. But I couldn't tell anyone, not even my best friend, Nina."—Jill, age 14

Like most people with bulimia, Amy hides her disorder well. She puts on a happy face. No one knows she's hurting inside. No one suspects she has an eating disorder.

Amy is of normal weight. She keeps her weight under control by purging. Amy has severe bulimia. She binges and purges an average of 14 times a week.

How Bulimia Can Begin

Amy began purging to try to keep her weight down. After she turned 16, she gained 15 pounds. That scared her. She figured it was because of her new job at the pizza restaurant. She would eat an entire large pizza at the end of her shift. She was so hungry she just couldn't help it.

Amy tried to diet, but she couldn't stick to it. After a few days of dieting, she'd be starved. She would start to eat and couldn't stop.

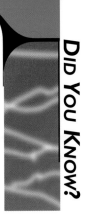
Hunger is a powerful binge trigger. The longer a person has dieted, the higher the risk of binge eating.

At first, Amy purged whenever she binged on food she thought was fattening. She would purge only once in a while. Later, purging became an uncontrollable urge. Eating any food, in any amount, triggered Amy's need to purge.

Amy used to binge on the spur of the moment. Later, she planned her binges. Sometimes she would consume up to 10,000 calories in one binge. (Adults generally consume 2,000 to 2,500 calories a day.) Amy usually purged by vomiting. Sometimes she used laxatives.

Food as a Comfort

Amy finds comfort in food. She feels satisfaction and relief in bingeing and purging. For people with bulimia, food often represents feelings they are trying to avoid or drive away. Bingeing and purging also can be a way for people who feel helpless or out of control to feel powerful. For them, having control over food makes them feel in control of their life.

Many people with bulimia are fascinated by food. They sometimes buy magazines and cookbooks to read recipes. They enjoy discussing diets.

However, bulimia is a two-headed monster. While people with bulimia find comfort in bingeing and purging, they also feel extreme guilt and shame. People with bulimia often try to hide their behavior from friends and family.

Bulimia is an addiction. Amy is addicted to the way she feels when she binges and purges. Like all addictions, bulimia is a way to run away from pain. Amy's bulimia is a sign that she is not facing her feelings.

Feeling Out of Control

People who have bulimia usually know their eating habits are not normal. They know their bulimia is a sign that something is wrong. Amy isn't proud that she is obsessed with keeping her weight down. She isn't happy with the way she is trying to control how her body functions. Amy is disgusted and ashamed of her eating habits. She knows that bingeing and purging is proof that she is not in control.

People with severe bulimia are amazed and horrified that they can't control their eating behavior. Like Amy, they usually need help to break the cycle of bingeing and purging.

"Why, why, why do I do this? I hate it. I hate throwing up. I'm scared. What if I die? I could die. What if one time my heart just stopped? Oh, God, I want to stop this throwing up before it kills me.

"Last night Kevin didn't call when he said he would. I don't know why. After dinner, I came up to my room and pulled out my stash of junk food. I stuffed cookies in my mouth so fast I was choking. My stomach was so full it felt like it would burst. I had to get that food out of me. So I made myself throw up. I always feel better at first, but then I start hating myself. I told myself I wouldn't do it again. But I know I will. All I think about is when I can binge and where and when I'll throw up."

Signs of bulimia:

Binge eating

Feeling out of control when eating

Vomiting, misusing laxatives, exercising, or fasting to get rid of calories

Dieting when not bingeing. Becoming hungry and bingeing again.

Believing being thin is important for self-worth

Being preoccupied with body weight and appearance

Having depression or mood swings

Shoplifting

Abusing alcohol, drugs, or credit cards

Points to Consider

Do you know anyone who has bulimia or whom you suspect has bulimia? How does that person behave?

Do you ever eat food because you're unhappy, bored, or afraid? Did eating make you feel better? Why or why not?

People with bulimia often feel ashamed of their bingeing and purging. Why do you think they feel ashamed?

Bingeing and purging harms the body.

Bulimia has mental, social, and emotional costs. People with bulimia may lose their ability to think logically. They may become anxious and irritable. They may isolate themselves from friends and family.

People with bulimia are at risk for developing impulsive behaviors such as sexual promiscuity and shoplifting. They also are at risk for substance abuse.

Bulimia can be treated and cured.

Chapter **5**

The Price of Bulimia

The teenage years hit LaRay
hard. She went from wearing
size 5 jeans to size 11. Her large breasts and hips made her
feel like everyone was staring at her. Boys made crude
remarks and laughed as she walked down the hall. LaRay
wanted one of those cute tank tops like her girlfriends were
wearing, but with her figure, how could she? She *had* to find
a way to lose weight.

How bulimia can affect you physically:

Rupture of the esophagus

Weakened resistance to illness and disease

Dental problems

Increased risk of heart disease

Hair growth on face, back, and arms

Disturbed sleep patterns

LaRay began dieting. She thought that losing weight would give her more confidence. She believed boys would like and respect her more if she were thin. When dieting didn't work, LaRay began bingeing and purging. Sadly, bulimia damaged her body, her friendships, and her self-esteem.

Physical Costs of Bulimia

Bingeing and purging harms the body in countless ways. Every organ and cell is affected. In extreme cases, death can result.

The strain of vomiting sometimes causes broken blood vessels in and around the eyes. It also can cause the saliva glands to swell. These appear as puffy areas below the corners of the mouth.

The stomach acid from vomiting can damage the mouth, teeth, throat, and esophagus. The tube that connects the throat and stomach can rupture, or burst, from acid created by throwing up. The acid from vomiting also wears away tooth enamel, paving the way for cavities to develop. Gums also may become diseased.

Fingers and knuckles can become bruised from forced vomiting. Bulimia can cause dry skin, brittle hair, and hair loss.

Purging causes the body to lose vitamins and minerals that are essential to good health. Laxatives can permanently change the function of the intestines.

In general, bingeing and purging wears the body down. Health declines, along with a person's strength, energy, and appearance.

Bulimia can be fatal. Purging can cause an electrolyte imbalance, which can result in a heart attack. Electrolytes are substances that help control a person's heartbeat.

Mental and Emotional Costs of Bulimia

Bingeing and purging takes a serious toll on a person's mental health. People with bulimia can lose the ability to think logically. They begin to believe they don't deserve to be happy or to get help for their problem.

How bulimia can affect you mentally:

Feeling out of control, helpless, and hopeless

Feeling anxiety, self-doubt

Fearing discovery

Having obsessive thoughts and compulsive behavior

Needing to control or suppress emotions

Feeling guilt and shame

A person with bulimia can slip into the destructive habit of lying. The person deceives friends and family about eating and vomiting, hiding food, or secretly using laxatives. This pattern can make the person with bulimia feel in control. In truth, people with bulimia may feel their lives are spinning out of control.

People with bulimia often are filled with anxiety and self-doubt. They may feel miserably unhappy but are helpless to make changes. They may feel guilty and ashamed about their behavior. Some may become depressed.

MINH, AGE 16

"I know Sylvie heard me vomiting. Now she's going to be after me. Or worse, she'll tell my mother.

"I can't go to her sleepover Friday night. What if I start eating and can't stop? I can't throw up in her apartment. Her whole family will hear.

"Besides, I'm so depressed, I don't want to go. I don't belong with that group. I know they think I'm boring and ugly."

Social Costs of Bulimia

Many people with bulimia are terrified of being found out. They tend to be suspicious of people who show interest or concern toward them. They may be afraid that these people will discover their secret.

People with bulimia may become more withdrawn and isolated, or separated, from family and friends. They often feel left out and lonely. They can end up with few, if any, satisfying relationships.

"How could you do it?" Daniel's mother screamed. "I can't believe you took those things. Shoplifting! What's wrong with you?"

DANIEL, AGE 14

Bulimia and Destructive Behavior

People with bulimia are at risk for dangerous impulsive behaviors. These include sexual promiscuity and shoplifting. Sexual promiscuity means having sexual relations with many different or unknown partners. In one study of people with bulimia, more than 40 percent had shoplifted, or stolen.

It is common for people with bulimia to be perfectionists. When they feel they have failed at something, they often punish themselves by bingeing and purging.

Research shows a relationship between bulimia and alcohol and drug abuse. One study of women with bulimia showed that a third abused alcohol. Another 28 percent abused other drugs. Of those, 18 percent overdosed repeatedly. In the same study, other types of self-destructive behaviors were common. These included self-cutting and stealing.

Bulimia can intensify a person's feelings of self-hate that lead to destructive behavior. Such behavior can endanger a person's life.

The Good News

Bulimia causes serious problems, but it is treatable. That's the good news. Recovery can be difficult, though. It can take a long time. For some it might take several months. For others it might take years. However long treatment takes, it is worth it. Recovery means health. It means winning back a person's life. The next chapter describes some of the ways bulimia is treated.

Points to Consider

What are some of the physical costs of bingeing and purging?

Why do you think people with bulimia are terrified of being found out?

Why do you think people with bulimia also might abuse drugs or alcohol or both?

Chapter Overview

Treatment for bulimia is different for each person. However, it always involves taking care of a person's physical and mental health.

Hospitalization can be necessary if body weight is extremely low or if bingeing and purging has severely affected a person's physical health.

A doctor, dentist, and nutrition counselor treat the physical health of a person with bulimia. Individual, family, and group therapists focus on improving the person's mental and emotional health.

Support groups provide encouragement, support, and practical advice.

Sometimes medications are helpful for relieving depression in people with bulimia.

Chapter **6**

Choosing Health

"When my mother found out about the bulimia, I was mad.
Maybe that was because I was so scared. I was really afraid I'd have to go into a hospital. I was so out of control. I got lucky, though. I could get treated at our clinic. I went to a therapist twice a week at first. My mom and I also saw the therapist together."

KARLA, AGE 18

Without treatment, up to 20 percent of people with serious eating disorders die. With treatment, that number falls to 2 to 3 percent.

Treating Bulimia

No one treatment works best for bulimia. The causes of bulimia are different for each person. The cures also are different. The best course is for a person to work with physicians and counselors. Usually any immediate physical problems resulting from bulimia are treated first. Then the causes of the person's bulimia—often emotional or psychological—can be addressed.

Dentists and physicians help deal with physical problems that result from bingeing and purging. They deal with such problems as dental disease or damage to organs. Counselors deal with psychological problems that are connected with bulimia, such as low self-esteem. Treatment may involve hospitalization, medical treatment, and nutrition counseling. It also may include therapy, support groups, and medications.

Hospitalization

Sometimes a person has such severe bulimia that he or she must be hospitalized. For a person who binges and purges several times a day, hospitalization may be the first step toward getting well. Immediate hospitalization is needed if a person blacks out or has chest pains. Other symptoms, or signs, requiring immediate hospitalization are tingling in hands or feet or vomiting uncontrollably.

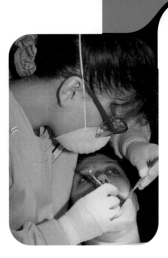

Some hospitals have units devoted to eating disorders. These units provide specialized medical and psychological care.

Medical Treatment and Nutrition Counseling

People with bulimia can do serious damage to their health. A doctor who is familiar with eating disorders can do a health assessment and prescribe treatment, if necessary. Sometimes a visit to a dentist may be required to determine if worn-away enamel has produced tooth decay.

Nutrition counselors help people with bulimia learn new ways to think about food and eating. They can help them develop healthful eating habits.

Individual, Family, and Group Therapy

Therapy is one of the most important tools in treating bulimia. All eating disorders are connected in some way to a person's emotional makeup.

In individual therapy, people with bulimia have a one-to-one relationship with a counselor or therapist. The therapist helps them discover why and how the eating disorder became their means of coping. With the help of the therapist, people with bulimia can learn new and healthier ways to cope.

Three important goals of individual therapy:

Express feelings

Learn how to accept uncertainty and change

Develop a strong sense of self and independence

Sometimes a person's eating disorder is a sign of family problems. Such problems can range from a family member's alcohol or drug use to difficulty communicating or expressing feelings. In family therapy, the therapist works with the person with bulimia and his or her family members. The family must be willing to participate in the therapy and to make changes in their own behavior. Otherwise, family therapy may not succeed.

In group therapy, the person with bulimia meets with other people who have eating disorders. A therapist leads the group. This type of therapy can help people realize they are not alone. Group members encourage each other. They help each other develop healthier eating and thought patterns.

FREDRIC, AGE 17

"Last night my parents had this horrible fight. It made me feel lousy. I wanted to eat in the worst way. I knew we had a gallon of ice cream. I really wanted to eat the whole thing. But I thought about what Jake had said at our last meeting. I told myself, 'Wait half an hour. You can do that. You can wait that long.' So I did. I waited half an hour. And guess what? I didn't care about eating anymore. Thanks, Jake. Thanks to all you guys."

Support Groups

Eating disorder support groups bring together people with similar problems. Groups can meet daily, weekly, or once a month. Usually a professional does not lead support groups. Members often pay little or nothing to attend. They talk about problems they are having and ways they deal with those problems. Like group therapy, support groups help people with bulimia realize they are not alone and that recovery is possible. Support groups can be a helpful addition to other therapy and medical care.

Medications

Medications have proven helpful in treating some people with bulimia. A doctor must write a prescription, or order, for such medications. Some antidepressants have helped relieve signs of severe depression and may lessen a person's need to binge and purge.

"It's hard for me to share my feelings. I was too ashamed and embarrassed to tell anyone what I was doing."—Anthony, age 16

"I tried for a long time to keep my bulimia a secret. I tried to stop on my own. It didn't work. I finally got help. My therapist told me most people with bulimia need help. It's too big a problem to deal with on their own. She's right. A lot of people are trying to help me get better."—Tami, age 18

Recovery Benchmarks

The most obvious sign of recovery for people with bulimia is that they no longer binge and purge. Here are more signs that indicate recovery:

Weight kept normal or near normal

Regular menstrual periods in females maintained

Healthful foods eaten in the right amount

Food no longer feared

Appropriate relationships maintained with family members

One or more satisfying friendships developed

Problem-solving skills improved

Interest shown in activities not related to food, weight, or appearance

Commitment made to making choices and living with consequences

Sense of self and goals developed

Realistic plan for achieving goals established

Points to Consider

Why do you think treatment is different for each person with bulimia?

Do you think all people with bulimia need medical treatment? Why?

Do you think all people with bulimia need some type of therapy? Why?

Explain why you agree or disagree with this statement: Getting the family involved is important to the recovery of a person with bulimia.

The most difficult step in treating bulimia is getting the person to admit a problem exists.

You can do many things to help a person who you suspect has bulimia. This includes being supportive, not talking about food and appearance, telling an adult you trust, and educating yourself.

You can help yourself if you suspect you have bulimia. You can change the way you talk to yourself, confide in someone you trust, and ask for help. You can learn all you can about bulimia.

Chapter **7**

What You Can Do

"Hey Sara! Can we talk a minute? I've been meaning to ask you about Dorina. Have you seen her lately? She barely said a word at lunch today. She never eats anymore, either. She told me she was on a diet. But then I saw a huge bag of chocolate bars in her backpack. I'm worried about her."

"I know, Cory. I'm worried, too. I swear I heard her throwing up in the bathroom the other day. Her eyes were watering and bloodshot when she came out of the stall. She won't talk to me either. I'm scared she's got bulimia."

Many people with bulimia do not admit they have a problem. This makes it difficult for others to help them. However, without help, most people with bulimia will not be able to break the cycle of bingeing and purging. Without help, they risk their health and their life.

If Someone You Know Needs Help

Many teens know or are acquainted with someone who has an eating disorder. Do you know someone who you think may have bulimia? Look again at the warning signs listed in chapter 4. What can you do to help?

First, it's important to understand that you cannot "fix" the person. Bingeing and purging is a symptom of other problems. The person is using bulimia as a way to cope.

The causes of bulimia are related to a person's psychological and emotional makeup. It is important for the person to deal with those issues first. Only then can the person's behavior be changed.

There are many things you can do to help a person who is dealing with bulimia. You can show you care. Talk with the person about your concern. Be a good listener. Feel free to talk about your own problems, too. This lets the person know he or she is not the only one with worries.

Here are a few other things you might do:

Avoid talking about weight and food. Don't point out how much the person eats. He or she needs your friendship, not criticism.

Avoid remarks about appearance. Instead, give compliments that have nothing to do with appearance. For example, say "Wow! You really did an awesome job on that report. The whole class was impressed."

Don't get discouraged. People with bulimia often don't trust others. You may feel rejected from time to time. However, don't give up. People who recover from bulimia credit their recovery most to a caring person in their life.

Talk about your concern with an adult you trust, such as the school nurse or guidance counselor. He or she might not be aware of the person's bulimia and may be able to help.

Educate yourself. The more you learn about bulimia, the more you can help. The For More Information section at the back of this book can help you.

You can offer support, but you can't cure the person's illness. Most people with bulimia need the help of trained professionals to get well.

"Be prepared. Your friend may get mad at you when you first approach her about your suspicion. She may say she doesn't have a problem. Don't push the issue. Just let her know you'll be there for her if she needs to talk."—Kelly, age 18

"Be careful what you say. Words hurt. Here are some of the things people said to me. 'You need to get your act together.' 'You're just doing this for attention.' 'I wish I could throw up all the food I eat. It would make things a lot easier.' Maybe they were trying to help, but they just made me feel worse."—Renata, age 15

If You Need Help

Perhaps you suspect you have bulimia. You have taken the first step toward a solution. Recognizing and admitting you may have a problem is the first step. People with bulimia often want to be helped.

The more you know about bulimia, the more you will be able to help yourself. You know that there are many causes of bulimia. The causes have a psychological and emotional basis. Some of those causes relate to the way you think about yourself.

You might try changing how you talk to yourself.

Here are some things you can say to yourself:

It's okay to worry.

It's okay to talk about my problems.

It's okay to have a good time.

I don't want food running my life.

I don't have to get on the scale every day.

I can figure out why I'm angry or sad.

I don't have to worry about what people think of me.

I can accept compliments.

I have many good qualities.

I don't have to be thin. Who says thin is beautiful, anyway? And who says they're right?

"I thought I was going nuts. The turning point in getting well for me was knowing someone understood how I felt. Mrs. Raymond, our school nurse, understood about my bulimia. She accepted it for what it was."
—Madison, age 16

"I knew I had to get well. But I couldn't have done it alone. I had one friend who stuck by me."
—Marty, age 15

"My mother confronted me one night. She was so mad. I'll never forget what she said. 'Yes, I'm angry. Yes, I'm frustrated. I'm angry because I love you. You're my daughter. You grew inside my body and now you're treating your own body with such contempt. It breaks my heart. You deserve so much better. How I wish you believed that.' I guess I did start believing it that night. That's when I decided I needed help."—Jana, age 17

You can do more than change your self-talk. Here are a few other suggestions:

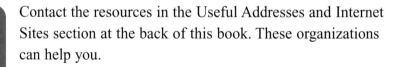

Contact the resources in the Useful Addresses and Internet Sites section at the back of this book. These organizations can help you.

Read the books suggested in the For More Information section at the back of this book.

Talk with someone you trust.

Don't be afraid to ask for help. It is a sign of strength, not weakness.

Know there are many people who can and want to help you.

Take one small step now. You will be glad you did!

Points to Consider

How would you help a friend who confided to you that he or she had bulimia?

Think of two adults you could talk with about bulimia. What would you say to them if you suspected a friend had bulimia?

Why is recognizing and admitting to a problem the first step in solving it?

Glossary

anxiety (ang-ZYE-uh-tee)—worry about something that might happen

cycle (SYE-kuhl)—an event or series of events repeated on a regular basis

destructive (di-STRUHK-tiv)—able to ruin completely or destroy

electrolyte (i-LEK-truh-lite)—a substance that is dissolvable and conducts electricity; in the body, electrolytes help regulate heartbeat.

enema (EN-uh-muh)—injection of liquid into the rectum to stimulate waste elimination

impulsive (im-PUHL-siv)—occurring on a whim or sudden urge

inherited (in-HER-it-uhd)—passed from parents to children; biological traits can be inherited.

intestine (in-TESS-tin)—a long tube extending below the stomach; the intestine digests food.

laxative (LAK-suh-tiv)—a medicine or food that helps make waste elimination happen quickly

nutrition (noo-TRISH-uhn)—food people need to eat to stay healthy

obsession (uhb-SESH-uhn)—an idea, thought, or emotion that is always on a person's mind

professional (pruh-FESH-uh-nuhl)—a person who is skilled in a certain field; a qualified expert.

psychological (sye-kuh-LOJ-uh-kuhl)—having to do with the mind or emotions

therapy (THER-uh-pee)—any procedure designed to improve a person's health or well-being

For More Information

Bode, Janet. *Food Fight.* New York: Simon & Schuster Books for Young Readers, 1997.

Burby, Liza. *Bulimia Nervosa: The Secret Cycle of Bingeing and Purging.* New York: Rosen, 1998.

Graves, Bonnie. *Anorexia.* Mankato, MN: Capstone Press, 2000.

Hornbacher, Marya. *Wasted: A Memoir of Anorexia and Bulimia.* New York: HarperCollins, 1998.

Schauss, Alexander. *Anorexia and Bulimia: A Nutritional Approach.* New Canaan, CT: Keats, 1997.

Sonder, Ben. *When Food Turns Against You.* New York: Franklin Watts, 1993.

Useful Addresses and Internet Sites

American Anorexia Bulimia Association
165 West 46th Street
New York, NY 10036
www.aabainc.org

Eating Disorders Awareness and Prevention
603 Stewart Street, Suite 803
Seattle, WA 98101

National Association of Anorexia Nervosa and
Associated Disorders (ANAD)
PO Box 7
Highland Park, IL 60035

The National Eating Disorders
Information Centre
200 Elizabeth Street, CW1-211
Toronto, Ontario M5G 2C4
CANADA
www.nedic.on.ca

Anorexia Nervosa and Related Eating
Disorders, Inc. (ANRED)
www.anred.com
Background, treatment, and recovery
information on topics related to eating
disorders

Eating Disorders Awareness and Prevention
(EDAP)
www.edap.org
Information about eating disorders, current
statistics, and prevention for all ages

Eating Disorders Shared Awareness (EDSA)
Canada: Mirror-Mirror
www.mirror-mirror.org/eatdis.htm
Resource in Canada for information on eating
disorders and recovery

Eating Disorders Shared Awareness (EDSA)
New York: Something Fishy
www.something-fishy.com
Information about eating disorders including
prevention, treatment, and recovery

Index

Index continued